Way Back Home

Philippa Ward

India | USA | UK

Way Back Home © 2022 Philippa Ward

All rights reserved.

No part of this publication may be
reproduced, stored in a retrieval system, or
transmitted, in any form or by any means,
electronic, mechanical, photocopying,
recording or otherwise, without the prior
written permission of the presenters.

Philippa Ward asserts the moral right to be
identified as author of this work.

Presentation by *BookLeaf Publishing*

Web: www.bookleafpub.com

E-mail: info@bookleafpub.com

ISBN: 9789357214803

First edition 2022

To Matt, who is the constant who has my back in all that I do, unconditionally and to my family, Maureen, John, Halo and Kaleb, who have always been my biggest cheerleaders.

ACKNOWLEDGEMENT

My lifelong love of words was nurtured by my father, who encouraged me to play with words and stretch my vocabulary whenever possible. My writing is a solitary process, until now I have chosen to keep it private. I like to shut myself away and meditate on the page as much as possible. It's my solace and my therapy. Apart from three friends, Richard, Deb and Sam, who have enthusiastically engaged in and encouraged my writing, there is nobody to thank except the fact that I'm alive and have lived. Life, my world within and the world around me have driven what lies in these pages.

PREFACE

This book has been waiting to exist for many decades, it is a purge of many years of deep thought and observations that needed to be harnessed and contained in tangible print. The words within have been cathartic and comforting to me and my only hope is that others can find meaning in these pages also.

Invidia

I must embrace my schadenfreude
So at odds with who I am
My cloak of lead, my sewn shut eyes
Selective blindness to what I have
I will question my karmic actions
I should ponder on deadly sin
I am a mass of contradictions
Toxic invidia has dyed my skin
Impure of heart, falling in envy
My palm engraved now with your name
Garden of statues is standing empty
My discontent, a bitter flame
Flawed and desiring, I seethe resentment
My peace of mind is emerald green
Fortune shines brightly but not on my face
The lack of everything that I have been
Now I must rest my tired ego
Duplicity, my double sides
I'll wear betrayal like a tuxedo
While I shall envy the seas you ride

The Lepidopterist

I look at you now
Encased behind glass
Immortalised forever
In a show built to last
Poised on a pin
In elegant repose
Iridescent colours
I remember those
A symbol of my freedom
A token of a love
A soft and gentle creature
Whose life was not enough
Many try to catch you
Ensnare you in their net
And though I have you in a box
I haven't caught you yet.

Earth Is Ours

3

Earth is ours in splendour complete
A broken bird's egg, scattered seed
Ruminations on a sunlit day
Thankful for the dazzling rays,
Hot as fire on my face

In whispering secrets passed through trees
Silent space where thoughts can cease
On spiralling spiderwebs laced with dew
Under canopies of verdant truth

Rain igniting hope of life
Spring's sweet cycle multiplies

Hummingbird

You conserve your energy
Let fragile wings unfurl
Hours away from starving
Bringing colour to this world

Not content in your torpor
You hover by the tree
Catch me on the upstroke
I marvel at your speed

Flying backwards for a while
No drop of nectar spilt
Your ruby throat content to drink
The tangled spider silk

Gleaming vivid colour
Naked to my eye
Wavelengths parting slowly
Beating wings to fly

Now you are left hollow
The downstroke wore you through
Until the sugar that you follow
Has resurrected you

If I Were Not A Woman

If I were not a woman, life would be more
simple

Instead I am a female predisposed to being
sinful

There'd be no copious bloodshed 13 weeks of
the year

No headaches, joint pains, acne, bloating or
diarrhoea

I wouldn't need to plan around a haemorrhage
once a month

The way it ruins everything with its crimson
sucker punch

If I were not a woman I'd be free from
imperfection

But when history says you're so much less, you
learn a harder lesson

Aristotle told us - we're inferior to men

He believed our blood was colder, that's what he
said back then

Subordinate - do not concern yourself with
brains or talent

Obey the father, husband, son, be small to keep
the balance

If I were not a woman, reproduction would be
easy

But agency in bodies isn't pertinent to my specie

I cannot simply tie the tubes like men can get the
snip

I'm valued for fertility and the bearing of my
hips

If I'm not making babies then exactly what am
I?

If I am unproductive, devoid, barren or sterile

If I were not a woman I could go out at night

Without fear of being followed if I don't stay in
the light

My skirts too short, my dress too tight, my heels
they say "fuck me"

So I shouldn't be surprised if I'm treated
shoddily

If I decide to wear clothes to accentuate my
shape

It's my fault if my evening out then culminates
in rape

If I were not a woman it would earn me higher
pay

The pink tax would not be mine and I could
have my say

If I were not a woman I could be in halls of
power

And not be judged on my looks which one day
will be soured

If I were not a woman maybe then they'd give
me funding

Instead of being sidelined and made to feel like
nothing

If I were not a woman I'd be more safe from
human traffic

Get to choose if I should wish to be in
something pornographic

If I were not a woman I'd less likely be harassed

Catcalled, fondled, groped and touched upon my
breasts and ass

If I were not a woman and considered second
class

Then maybe I'd love myself more and not put
myself last

But here I am, a woman and I really am quite
jealous

That because I was born female they think I'll
feed their bellies

Do all the chores and work, tend and clean and
cook and care

And things look very different when I cannot be
there

And if I do not do it then… I feel all of the guilt

Because I am the dutiful woman that this society
built

Lilith

They say you have a destructive nature
But I know it's your dead despair
They say they hear your errant laughter
Echoing on midnight air
They think they know how your story goes
But they don't see your buried woes
They cast you far beyond the stones
They do not hear your swallowed words

Your castle's overgrown by thorns
Your reputation met with scorn
Sent the angels to retrieve you
Lilith - why won't they believe you?

Lilith you are every woman
That ever dared say no
Lilith you are every woman
That has dared to grow
If you were male they'd call you brave
Their cups would overflow
But Lilith you are every woman,
Every woman that I know

You know how to stop your heart from bleeding
You know your time is fleet

You don't want perfection of Eden
It's not the way to find your peace
Beauty and pain are in your silence
Your separation leaves clean wounds
Refusal to submit, your defiance
Moods bloom by breaking rules

And they say that you weaken
The children of men
That you give birth to demons
Then they leave you condemned...
Lilith you are every woman
Every woman that I've known

Magenta

Battle of Magenta, banned from borders
Derided, shunned, stigmatised, the floral original
sin
London Purple, poison, arsenic, peril and
pollution
Beware the hues of crimson, the aniline illusion
Don Quichotte Triumph Tulip, firework
explosion
Perfume of the roses, vibrant summer phlox
Fuschine, majestic Trumpet Flowers, colour run
amok
Covering ground in vital waves, a lustrous ocean
Now resurrected, pardoned, restored in
splendour
Neon bright abundance, planted in good measure
Shimmering fruit of Beautyberry, jewels in
buried treasure
Lily Flowered Purple Dream, riot of colour
tender
Social complexities embedded in our gardens
Echoes of a time anxious of a changing world
Embraced again now fear has passed,
Granted now a pardon

Pluvophile

Rebellious mist over outstretched land

Mystic, wild spirit earth

Darkening skies bring drenching rain

Storm winds reaping peace of mind

A pluvophile finds comfort here

In beating pit-pat, tapping fingers

Amethyst drops on window pain

Sheets of slanting silvery rain

Restoring and igniting life

Roots grow deeper, flower heads bow

Cleansing earth and thirsty ground

Therapeutic is the sound

Beady drops on glistening bough

Plopping raindrops on the river

Making circles on the surface

Some find rain so fierce and fitful

Inconvenient, desolate

I look forward to downpours imminent

Revitalising, rhythmic joy

Peaceful song of happiness

Self Saboteur

15

I do not want to talk

You might just tell me lies

The weight of insecurity

Lays heavy on my mind

I do not want to feel

As feeling causes pain

And if I practise numbness

Normalcy's easier to feign

I do not want to sleep

The new day will come faster

I'll stay awake until I'm sick

And ward off the next chapter

I do not want to go outside

Relinquish my control

I'll stay in here, my coast is clear

And I won't see a soul

I do not want to live

It's fraught with complications

And staying small is my downfall

But it's damage limitation

I do not want to die

I've feared it all my life

I won't end it all but if it calls

I won't put up a fight

Loneliness

Loneliness hides in a deafening crescendo

Of compulsory comparisons

Be beautiful

Be successful

Be out there

Neither valid nor validated

Loneliness is emptiness, the suffocation of a
heart

Stepping on loose soil

Falling into a pit

Becoming an echo

They won't cry for long

Forgotten but unforgotten

The list of "things to do" continues

Life's relentless march within you

Sadness overrides the energy

Numbness, stiffness,

To do, to live

Breathing but not breathing

Veneer

Falling over me like a veil
No warning signs just blaring alarms
Can't fight it at all
Taking my power and hope
I watch life from the periphery
With the detachment of a professional
Losing count of the times
It's stolen my joy

Cut off from reality
A stranger to myself
Where do I go?
Who should I be?
Who can I trust?
Who can trust me?
Locked in, I'm a prisoner
Of my emotional extremes

If I were brave enough I'd fight
With chemical weapons
A noose or a knife
I'd lock it down tight
But I create a veneer
Posture and pretend
Adjusting my mask

While I take flight again

There's a frequency, a regularity
That it visits me
Here it comes again
Swooping stealth
The hunter and the prey
Rinsed in pain
Continue to hide
While I crumble inside

Jonestown

Oh you were a troubled one
Captured by obsessions
Religion, death and tyrants
Leading by impression

Inspired by the wrong one
The evil of before
Castles of paranoia
Selling monkeys door to door

Moved out to eureka
Just west of the sierras
Built the people's temple
A place of leave me never

There you gave your soft sell
For higher evolution
Wave after wave they came to you
Seeking their solutions

Attracted by the people
Where colour was no object
Father divine preacher
Mind control of loyal subjects

Still they came in hundreds
Women, men and children
Your infallible Valhalla
Duplicity still building

Then one day, stone by stone,
All you had to do was ask
They drank your saved up cyanide
Lay face down on the grass

Singing take me to the heaven's gate
Show me new reality
Make me drink that punch of lace
That blessed potency

Women, men and children
Children, women, men
The right thing in the wrong place
A dark and bitter end

Words

There's comfort in words
The blank of a page
Enticing, inviting me
To purge my malaise
I can empty my head
Of bother and strife
When I sit to record
The minutiae of life
Cleansing and healing
To empty my soul
Cleaning the cobwebs
My ultimate goal
Some think me obsessive
This peculiar trait
My pedantic tendency
To write notes on my fate
But I feel it a privilege
My great need to scribe
To read back through my words
And know I'm alive

Angels in Exile

Sweet boys, so beautiful and damned
Secrets deep inside few will understand
Can't show their love, can't give their names
Fighting a war and not coming back the same
These aches that they feel
The pain beyond measure
Pain today that was yesterday's pleasure

Late night cabarets, no rest in their hearts
Desires and dreams so beautifully flawed
Loves and lives no freedom of choice
Not every love is given a voice
Seeing them rise, watching them fall
Questions in silence or asked not at all

Family home seemed so far from Heaven
Lives lived but worked to keep hidden
Unspoken words bleeding from fingers
Invisible wounds, sorrows that linger
Walking in beauty so far from home
Bitter winds chiming like ice in the bone

A storm not heard until it breaks
Silhouettes of regret and foolish mistakes
Like finds like and each stone in the well

Has a tale not to tell
Such a tale not to tell

Angels in exile, faces under glass
Drifting histories of friends who have passed
A last chance saloon of a flower not to bloom
Left alone in a room
Angels in exile, scratchings in stone
Angels in exile so far from their homes
Beautiful lives,
Once here,
But denied,
The tender gift,
Of time

Wishes

They were a certain kind of person
Who crept around their world
Watching life from all the corners
Until their edges curled
Uncertain, sad, lonely
Cautious and so fearful
Walking the peripheries,
Keeping it provincial

They wrote down all their wishes
Kept them in a bag
A hundred different hopes and dreams
Borne of a private iliad
Wrapped up tight in a velvet pouch
Their secret mayday flag
Daydreaming like a curious child
Of plans to breathe and laugh

Longing for another
To share their fragile days
Someone who would love them
Accept their abstract ways
Every day they'd hide away
Right out there in plain sight
And watch the passing strangers

As they hid their shining light

On a park somewhere in England
They sat most every day
Always in the same spot
Under the birch tree's sway
Artfully undercover,
Forever dressed in black
On the bench that bore the golden plaque
Of someone's epitaph

Seasons passed, time marched on
A hole wore in the bag
One of their wishes trickled free
Out in the world it sat
A passer by, a kindred soul
Picked it up and read the words
They'd never felt so seen,
They'd never felt so heard

"Does this belong to you"? They asked
"Can I sit by you please?"
"I've been waiting my life long
For someone just like me
Can I spend a moment,
Share the contents of my heart?
Your wish is mine, it's intertwined,
I hoped - now here you are"

Kisses After Every Fall (for my children)

I remember when I began counting time
When my body knitted you together
The starring role of my lifetime
A love bond to bind us forever
I remember when my soul was divided
When my existence profoundly changed
Everything I knew was redefined
Acting on a different stage
You came along, my heart was bared
It beats outside my chest
Night after night and day by day
Beating without rest
All those nights spent dancing without a beat
Your head on my chest I rocked you to sleep
Singing solo like a dream walked in a field
Holding past and future in each moment

Born to a clear path, now you've grown
Spent my strength steering this life's work of my
own
You look at me now, my babies in your eyes
Still the one that you call home
I'm here for you, every hurt to cure
I will soothe them all

Here for you with a love that's pure
With kisses after every fall
And though your hands are no longer small
I will hold them through it all
With kisses after every fall
Kisses after every fall

Where the Sun Shines

Music was my first love, the soundtrack to my
life
And there's a certain sound that always makes
my day more bright
It comes from the west coast and way back in
the day
It was known as AOR boosted by FM radio play
It's called a guilty pleasure now but I Can't Go
For That
The music known as Yacht Rock is where the
sunshine's at
With smooth soul, jazzy riffs, a touch of R'n'B
Some funk and disco, high production, catchy
melodies
Feel good songs of foolish men, elite players by
the ounce
Electric piano exhilarates that upbeat Doobie
Bounce
Aspirational escape, words complex and wry
Keep it smooth even when it grooves, bringing
in the light
So I'll sip a Pina Colada and then I'll Hold The
Line
On a sound that will transport me back to
another time

The Visitor

My name is one that many know, I don't
discriminate
I could visit any one of you, one in 5 or 6 or 8
Since dawn of humankind, I've really got around
But there's misunderstanding of where I can be
found

In times gone by and some today, thought me
supernatural
Work of the devil, good or evil or merely
biological?
Sorcery or witchcraft, genie, seer or sage
The prejudice has shifted through each and
every age

Socrates was not exempt, he had hallucinations
Pythagoras heard voices which were all of my
creation
The Romans thought the moon caused where the
madness led them
Then mass delusion, witch hunts, workhouse,
poorhouse, back to Bedlam

It wasn't till last century that things began to
change

Now still there is work to be done, don't think of
me as strange
There's been a shift, how I'm perceived, a
change within the language
But still there is suspicion when I come to cause
you anguish

I still have power to derail, to destroy and to
shame
Let there be no judgment on the lives that I have
claimed
For all those who still suffer and for those I've
taken down
For those who stumble, fall or freeze when I
have come around,
It's time to stop the stigma, it's time to talk the
truth
My name is mental illness, I'll visit any one of
you

Delve Deeper (Question Everything)

Tap below the surface
Look at the inside
Don't rely on outer casing
Think about what hides
Beware a glossy cover
Which promises much more
Reject the superficial
Get right to the core
Peel back all the layers
Burrow under skin
Count the rings inside the trunk
Seek out what's within
No one shows their everything
Don't make your mind up yet
Never take for granted
That what you see is what you get

Free Verse (Not!)

The problem with my writing is finding where to
start
A page lies there before me, waiting for the art
So many styles to choose from, if I have the time
My only issue is, I'm compelled to make it
rhyme
I want to write in free verse or some romantic
sonnet
A villanelle or elegy, something so symbolic
I aspire to pen an epic of exciting, wild
adventures
Then fail to create anything that doesn't feel
pretentious
A haiku would be refreshing or an ode to change
my game
But my brain is trained and is enslaved to words
that sound the same
When I sit here of a morning, trying to be poetic
The rhyming words flow out of me -
unapologetic
So let it be one day written upon my epitaph,
"Pippa drowned in a sea of rhyme, here lies the
aftermath!"

Greatest Hits of Gross

Do you like the word gusset? I wagered you
would not
I put it here to test you out, see if it hit the spot
Welcome to my thoughts...subject: word
aversion
To ponder the topic of the words that cause
people diversion
There's maggot, gurgle, phlegm and curd, squirt,
orifice and munch
There's crevice, navel, puke and scab in this
repulsive bunch
The list of words that do perturb or cause folk
such an issue
Evocative of matters that need mopping up with
tissue
The one that seems a winner, that would be most
people's choice
Is irrational distaste for the sound of the word
moist
A word that advertisers have removed from the
marketplace
As the visceral reactions saw it sent off in
disgrace
Which collection of such letters makes you want
to hurl?

When words and meaning's arbitrary what
makes your toes curl?
Which would cause a freak out like Monty
Python's Flying Circus?
Is it bulbous, pustule, ooze or smear, pus, fudge
or even mucus?
We all have linguistic foibles, it's base
psychology
There will be strong reactions to this yuck
anthology
So which words cause you outrage? Which do
you hate the most?
And is it here, included, in my greatest hits of
gross?